IS-201: Forms Used for the Development of the Incident Action Plan

By

Fema

10/31/2013

IS-201: Forms Used for the Development of the Incident Action Plan

Lesson 1: Course Introduction

Course Purpose

Welcome to the *IS-201: Forms Used for the Development of the Incident Action Plan* course.

The purposes of this course are:

- To provide participants with an overview of standard ICS forms and an opportunity to review their application within the incident action planning process.
- To provide emergency response personnel and incident command practitioners with renewed awareness of and basic information on the use and completion of recently published FEMA All-Hazards ICS forms for incident management and coordination activities.

Course Overview

- Are designed to serve all-hazards, cross-disciplinary needs for incident management across the Nation
- Include the essential data elements for the ICS process they address
- Create a foundation within the ICS for complex incident management activities
- Are intended for use as tools to assist in the creation of Incident Action Plans (IAPs), for other incident management activities, and for support and documentation of ICS activities

Throughout this course, the purpose for, preparation of, and distribution of the ICS forms are written in accordance with the FEMA Forms Book 502-2. This document can be downloaded from: https://www.fema.gov/national-incident-management-system/incident-command-system-resources.

Course Objectives

At the end of this course, you should be able to:

- Describe the process by which the IAP is developed and implemented, using ICS forms, consistent with the Planning "P"
- Identify the uses of ICS-201, ICS-211, and ICS 214 in the incident command system
- Identify the purpose, preparation, and distribution of the information captured on ICS-215 and ICS-215A, and describe the relationship of this information to other ICS forms commonly used in composing an IAP
- Identify the purpose, preparation, and distribution of, and describe the relationship of, the information captured on the ICS-202, ICS-203, ICS-204, ICS-205, and ICS-206 forms relative to an IAP
- Identify the purpose of the ICS supplementary forms, such as ICS-208 (Safety Message/Plan), ICS-213 (General Message), and ICS-221 (Demobilization Check-Out), needed to assist with information collection and dissemination during an incident
- Describe the importance of a demobilization plan

Lesson 2: ICS Forms and the Planning "P"

Introduction

Welcome to Lesson 2, ICS Forms and the Planning "P". At the conclusion of this lesson, you will be able to:

- Describe the process by which the IAP is developed and implemented, using ICS forms, consistent with the Planning "P".

Notice to all NIMS ICS All-Hazards Position-Specific and IS-201 ICS Forms Class Students:

The Planning Cycle, or "Planning 'P'" as it's generally referred to, establishes a continuum for Incident Action Planning (IAP) during both emergency and non-emergency operations. The Planning "P" as defined in the Planning "P" video is an integral tool for the NIMS ICS All-Hazards Position-Specific coursework. The Planning "P" used in that coursework and video is a slight modification of the Planning "P" identified in NIMS, which is used in this course.

The timing of the Command and General Staff meeting, as noted on the Planning "P", accounts for the difference in the planning cycles. NIMS places this meeting between the Incident Command/Unified Command Develop/Update Objectives Meeting and the Preparing for the Tactics Meeting. The Planning "P" used in the previously mentioned coursework and the video recognizes the flexibility of the Command and General Staff meeting, and relies on the needs of the incident to determine the timing for the meeting.

Lesson Introduction (continued)

The Incident Action Plan (IAP):

- Is defined as an oral or written plan containing general objectives reflecting the overall strategy for managing an incident
- May include the identification of operational resources and assignments
- May include attachments that provide direction and important information for management of the incident
- Should be considered a work in progress during the initial stages of incident response

Planning Process Overview

Sound, timely planning provides the foundation for effective incident management. The planning process represents a template for strategic, operational, and tactical planning that includes all steps that an Incident Command/Unified Command (IC/UC) and other members of the Command and General Staff should take to develop and disseminate an IAP.

The planning process may begin with the:

- Scheduling of a planned event
- Identification of a credible threat
- Initial response to an actual or impending incident

The process continues with the implementation of the formalized steps and the staffing required for the development of a written IAP.

Planning Process: Five Primary Phases

The five primary phases should be followed in sequence to ensure a comprehensive IAP. These phases are designed to enable the accomplishment of incident objectives within a specified time.

The primary phases of the planning process are essentially the same for the IC who develops the initial plan, for the IC and Operations Section Chief revising the initial plan for extended operations, and for the Incident Management Team (IMT) developing a formal IAP.

The five primary phases are:

1. Analyze the Situation, Including Future Developments
2. Establish Incident Objectives and Strategy
3. Develop the Plan
4. Prepare and Disseminate the Plan
5. Execute, Evaluate, and Revise the Plan

1. Analyze the Situation, Including Future Developments

The first phase includes gathering, recording, analyzing, and displaying situation, resource, and incident-potential information in a manner that will facilitate:

- An ICS-201 or other initial incident tracking resource, such as a status board or jurisdiction-specific forms, which are often used to capture initial incident command objectives, resource status, and immediate actions and may be used to provide an initial briefing for additional command personnel
- The ability to determine the resources committed and those that may be required, including Command and General Staff who may be needed to develop and implement an effective IAP

- Increased situational awareness of the magnitude, complexity, and potential impact of the incident

This phase is the vertical leg of the Planning "P".

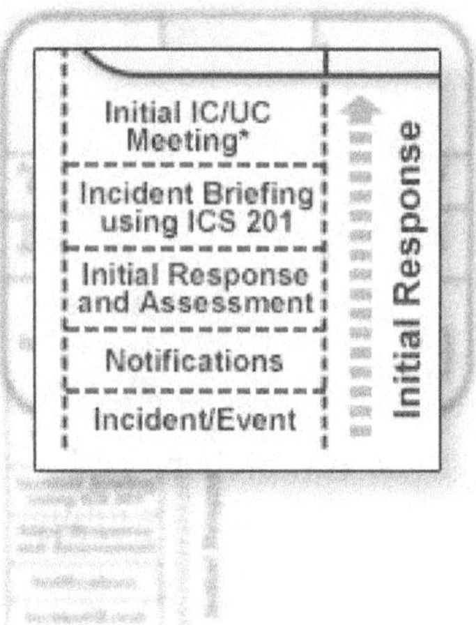

2. Establish Incident Objectives and Strategy

The second phase includes formulating and prioritizing SMART incident objectives and identifying appropriate strategies to meet incident challenges (ICS-215 and ICS-215A).

SMART objectives are:

- **S**pecific—what exactly are we going to do, with whom, and for whom?
- **M**easurable—is it measurable and how do WE measure it?
- **A**ction-Oriented—what are the performance expectations?
- **R**ealistic—can it be accomplished as proposed?
- **T**ime frame—when will we accomplish this objective?

Within the Planning "P", this is the phase when the IC/UC develop the initial incident objectives or revise the incident objectives for the next operational period.

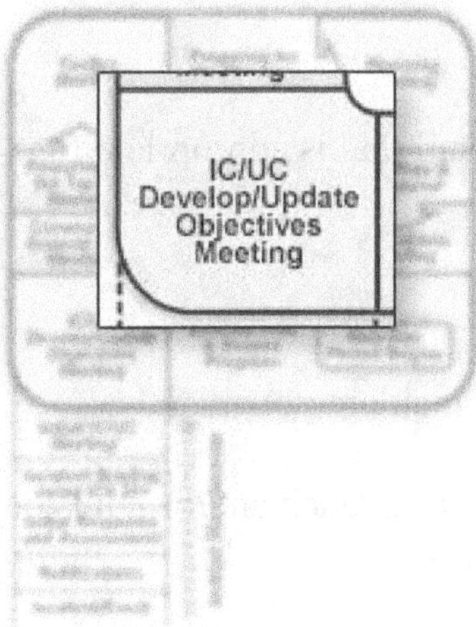

3. Develop the Plan

The third phase involves determining the tactical direction and the specific resources, reserves, and support requirements for implementing the selected strategies and tactics for the operational period (ICS-215, ICS-215A, ICS-202, ICS-203, ICS-204, ICS-205, ICS-206).

This phase in the Planning "P" includes a meeting of the Command and General Staff, with each position making a determination as to what they forecast, how they prioritize their resource needs, and how they will achieve specific objectives. This is the preparation for the Planning Meeting to finalize the IAP.

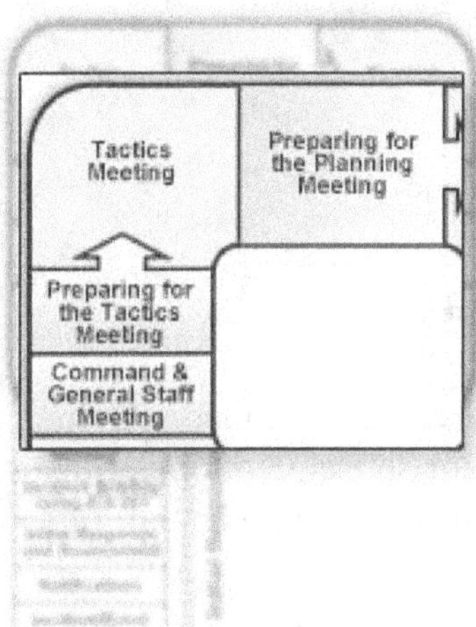

4. Prepare and Disseminate the Plan

The fourth phase involves preparing the plan to include the detail that is appropriate for the level of complexity of the incident.

Within the Planning "P", this step includes:

- Giving an update on the situation, resource status, and incident potential
- Reviewing and reconfirming objectives
- Identifying geographic operational lines, establishment of Branch and/or Division boundaries, and identifying functional Group assignments
- Assigning specific tactics for each Division and/or Group
- Identifying operational facilities and reporting locations
- Confirming resource orders
- Communications, Medical, and Traffic Plan requirements and considerations
- Finalization, approval, and implementation of the IAP

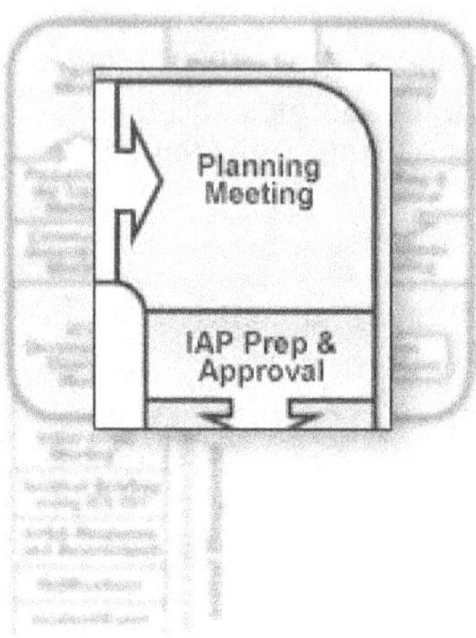

5. Execute, Evaluate, and Revise the Plan

The planning process includes the expectation to execute and evaluate planned activities and check the accuracy of information to be used in planning for subsequent operational periods. The General Staff should regularly compare planned progress with actual progress during the operational period.

Within the Planning "P", this phase of the planning process is the lower right corner and bottom half, which now completes the Planning "P" and the operational period in which it was used.

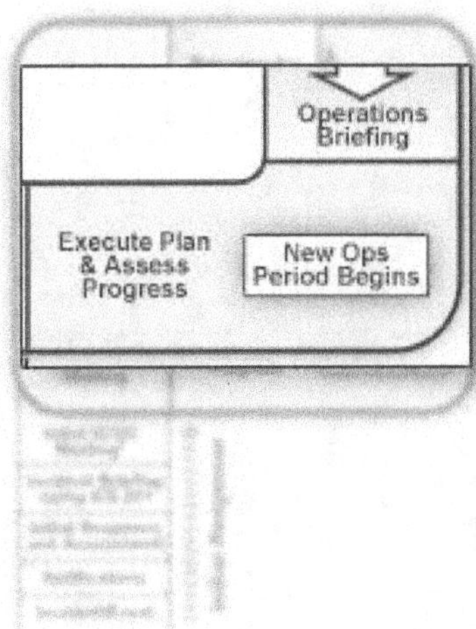

Lesson Summary

- During all stages of incident management, planners should gather, assess, and disseminate information
- ICS forms are valuable tools to assist in developing a simple plan that can be communicated through briefings
- Frequently, the initial plan must be developed very quickly and with incomplete situation information
- Using the ICS forms to gather information provides a template for strategic, operational, and tactical planning

Lesson 3: Initial Planning Information and ICS Forms

Introduction

Welcome to Lesson 3, Initial Planning Information and ICS Forms. At the conclusion of this lesson, you will be able to:

- Identify the uses of an ICS-201 (Incident Briefing), ICS-211 (Resource Check-In), and ICS 214 (Unit Log)

ICS Forms 201, 211, and 214 Overview

The ICS-201, ICS-211, and ICS-214 forms allow for:

- The capture of vital incident information
- A concise documentation of resources on-scene and the actions taken by those resources

ICS-201: Incident Briefing

Purpose: The Incident Briefing (ICS 201) provides the IC (and the Command and General Staff) with basic information regarding the incident situation and the resources allocated to the incident. This form may be used by the initial IC. Once the incident/event begins, the information used for the steps within the Planning "P", Notifications, Initial Response and Assessment, and the Incident Briefing, may be gathered using ICS-201. In addition, it may be used to facilitate the oral briefing in the transfer of command process.

Preparation: The briefing form is prepared by the initial IC for presentation to the incoming IC, along with a more detailed oral briefing.

Distribution: This form is designed to be transferred easily to the members of the Command and General Staff as they arrive and begin work.

ICS-211: Incident Check-In List

Purpose: Personnel and equipment arriving at the incident can check in at various incident locations. Check-in consists of reporting specific information, which is recorded on the Check-In List (ICS-211). It serves the following purposes:

- Records arrival times at the incident of all overhead personnel, tactical resources, and equipment
- Records the initial location of personnel and equipment to facilitate subsequent assignments
- Supports demobilization by recording the home base, method of travel, etc. for resources checked in

Preparation: This can be done at the check-in location at the Incident Command Post (ICP) or at various other locations, such as staging areas, bases, or camps.

Distribution: ICS-211s are kept by the Resources Unit in the Planning Section (if established) and shared with the Demobilization Unit and Finance/Administration Section. The Resources Unit maintains a master list of all equipment and personnel that have arrived at the incident.

ICS-214: Activity Log

Purpose: The Activity Log (ICS-214) records details of notable activities at any ICS level, including single resources, equipment, task forces, etc. These logs should be kept at all times for providing basic incident activity documentation, and as a reference for any after-action report. In addition, this form can assist the Time Unit, Cost Unit, and Compensation and Claims Unit in providing accurate reports to other agencies after the incident to document reimbursement claims.

Preparation: An ICS-214 can be initiated and maintained by personnel in various ICS positions as needed or appropriate. Personnel should document how relevant incident activities are occurring and progressing, as well as any notable events or communication. The ICS-214 must be maintained by all supervisors.

Distribution: Completed ICS-214s are submitted to supervisors, who forward them to the Documentation Unit. All completed original forms must be given to the Documentation Unit, which maintains a file of all ICS-214s. It is recommended that individuals retain a copy for their own records.

Lesson Summary

ICS forms 201, 211, and 214 are important and should be completed and distributed among the various Command and General Staff positions. These forms should be used to:

- Gather information
- Provide a quick look at the resources on hand or to be ordered
- Begin to create a common operating picture to develop situational awareness

All of these are the first steps within the Planning "P" for the development of the IAP.

Lesson 4: Starting the Incident Action Plan: ICS-215 and ICS-215A

Introduction

Welcome to Lesson 4, Starting the Incident Action Plan: ICS-215 and ICS-215A. At the conclusion of this lesson, you will be able to:

- Identify the purpose of, the preparation and distribution of, and describe the relationship of the information captured on ICS-215 and ICS-215A to other ICS forms commonly used in composing an IAP

ICS Forms 215 and 215A Overview

The ICS-215 and ICS-215A are valuable tools to document information for preparing the IAP. They are virtually essential to identifying the supervisory organization, tactical assignments, and resource needs to satisfy the operational objectives established by the IC/UC and to identify potential safety risks that may disrupt any tactical activities.

While not actually a part of the IAP, completed ICS-215 and ICS 215A documentation provides the core data needed to prepare other ICS forms that are components of an IAP.

ICS-215 Form and the Planning "P"

This form is used in the second step of the five Primary Planning Phases known as "Establish Incident Objectives and Strategy" and is found in the Planning "P" at the IC/UC Develop/Update Objectives Meeting.

This step includes:

- Formulating and prioritizing measurable incident objectives and identifying an appropriate strategy
- Identifying, analyzing, and evaluating reasonable strategies to determine the most appropriate strategy for the situation at hand
- Evaluating criteria, including public health and safety factors, estimated costs, and various environmental, legal, and political considerations

ICS-215: Operational Planning Worksheet

Purpose: The Operational Planning Worksheet (ICS-215) communicates the decisions made by the Operations Section Chief during the Tactics Meeting concerning resource assignments and needs for the next operational period.

Preparation: The ICS-215 is initiated by the Operations Section Chief and often involves logistics personnel, the Planning Section Chief, and the Safety Officer. The form is shared with the rest of the Command and General Staff in preparing for the Planning Meeting.

Distribution: When the Branch, Division, or Group work assignments and accompanying resource allocations are agreed upon, the form is distributed and used by the Planning Section to assist in the preparation of the ICS-204. The Logistics Section will use a copy of this worksheet for preparing requests for resources required for the next operational period.

ICS-215A: Incident Action Plan Safety Analysis

Purpose: The purpose of the Incident Action Plan Safety Analysis (ICS-215A) is to aid the Safety Officer in completing an operational risk assessment to prioritize hazard, safety, and health issues, and to develop appropriate mitigations. This worksheet is best used in the planning phase to identify safety concerns for all operational assignments.

Preparation: The ICS-215A is typically prepared by the Safety Officer during the incident action planning cycle. When the Operations Section Chief is preparing for the Tactics Meeting, the Safety Officer collaborates with the Operations Section Chief to complete the form. This form is closely linked to the Operational Planning Worksheet (ICS-215).

Distribution: When the safety analysis is completed, the form is distributed to the Resources Unit to help prepare ICS-204 forms for each Branch, Division, and Group. All completed forms must be given to the Documentation Unit in the Planning Section.

Lesson Summary

The ICS-215 Operational Planning Worksheet is used to:

- Determine geographic (Division) or functional (Group) assignments
- Establish the specific work assignments (Tactics) to be performed during the next operational period

- Determine the resources needed to accomplish the work assignments

ICS-215A Incident Action Plan Safety Analysis form is used to:

- Produce an operational risk assessment in order to prioritize hazards, safety, and health issues, and develop appropriate control
- Enable Command and General staff to form a complete picture in anticipation of planned operational activities

Lesson 5: Preparation and Application of the Incident Action Plan

Introduction

Welcome to Lesson 5, Preparation and Application of the Incident Action Plan. At the conclusion of this lesson, you will be able to:

- Identify the purpose of, the preparation and distribution of, and describe the relationship of the information captured on the ICS-202, ICS-203, ICS-204, ICS-205, and ICS-206 forms relative to an IAP

Forms Overview

All of the forms presented in this lesson are integral parts of the IAP that describes:

- What must be done—Incident Objectives (ICS-202)
- Who is responsible—Organization Assignment List (ICS-203) and Assignment List (ICS-204)
- How information will be communicated—Communications Plan (ICS-205 and ICS-205A)
- What should be done if someone is injured—Medical Plan (ICS-206)

ICS-202: Incident Objectives

Purpose: The Incident Objectives (ICS-202) form describes the incident objectives, command emphasis/priorities, and safety considerations for the next operational period.

Preparation: The ICS-202 is completed by the Planning Section following each Command and General Staff meeting conducted to prepare the IAP.

Distribution: The ICS-202 is generally the first page of the IAP and given to all supervisory personnel at the Section, Branch, Division/Group, and Unit levels. All completed forms must be given to the Documentation Unit in the Planning Section.

ICS-203: Organization Assignment List

Purpose: The Organization Assignment List (ICS-203) provides a list of all primary supervisors, from Command and General staff to subordinate supervisor staff. It is used to complete the Incident Organization Chart (ICS-207), which is posted on the Incident Command Post display.

Preparation: The Planning Section prepares and maintains this list under the direction of the Planning Section Chief.

Distribution: The ICS-203 is duplicated and attached to the Incident Objectives (ICS-202) form and given to all recipients as the second page of the IAP. All completed forms must be given to the Documentation Unit in the Planning Section.

ICS-204: Assignment List

Purpose: The Assignment List (ICS-204) informs Division and Group supervisors of incident assignments. Once the Command and General Staff agree to the assignments, the assignment information is given to the appropriate Divisions and Groups.

Preparation: Each ICS-204 is normally prepared by the Planning Section using the incident objectives from the Incident Objectives form (ICS-202), Operational Planning Worksheet (ICS-215), and Incident Safety Analysis Worksheet (ICS-215A.). It must be approved by the Incident Commander.

Distribution: The ICS-204 is part of the IAP. In some cases, assignments may be communicated via radio/telephone/fax. All completed original forms must be given to the Documentation Unit. A separate ICS-204 should be prepared for each assignment captured on the ICS-215 (and ICS-215A) to provide specific tactical assignments to Branches, Divisions, and Groups. Division/Group supervisors will assign more detailed tasking orders to strike teams, task forces, and single resources.

ICS-205: Incident Radio Communications Plan

Purpose: The Incident Radio Communications Plan (ICS-205) provides information on all radio frequency or trunked radio system talkgroup assignments for each operational period.

Preparation: The ICS-205 is prepared by the Logistics Section and given to the Planning Section Chief for inclusion in the IAP.

Distribution: The ICS-205 is part of the IAP. All completed forms must be given to the Documentation Unit. Information from the ICS-205 is placed on the Assignment List (ICS-204). The FEMA Forms Book 502-2 provides an ICS-205a (Communications List) that contains a list of wireless/telephone communications for all supervisors.

ICS-206: Medical Plan

Purpose: The Medical Plan (ICS-206) provides information on incident medical aid stations, transportation services, hospitals, and medical emergency procedures primarily for incident response resources.

Preparation: The ICS-206 is prepared by the Logistics Section and reviewed by the Safety Officer to ensure ICS coordination. If aviation assets are used for rescue, coordination with the Air Operations branch is required.

Distribution: The ICS-206 is part of the IAP. All completed forms must be given to the Documentation Unit in the Planning Section.

Lesson Summary

- ICS-202: Incident Objectives – describes the basic incident strategies, objectives, command emphasis or priorities, and safety considerations
- ICS-203: Organizational Assignment List – provides a full accounting of incident management and supervisory staff for that operational period
- ICS-204: Assignment List – details the specific actions the Divisions or Groups will be taking in support of the overall incident objectives
- ICS-205: Incident Radio Communications Plan – provides information on all radio frequency assignments down to the Division/Group level for each operational period
- ICS-206: Medical Plan – provides information on incident medical aid stations, medical transportation, hospital, and medical emergency procedures for response resources

A completed IAP must have an ICS-202, ICS-203, and ICS-204 for each division and group. The ICS-205 (Communications Plan) and ICS-206 (Medical Plan) may not be required in all cases.

Lesson 6: Supplemental ICS Forms and Demobilization

Introduction

Welcome to Lesson 6, Supplemental ICS Forms and Demobilization. At the conclusion of this lesson, you will be able to:

- Identify the purpose of the ICS supplemental forms, such as ICS-208 (Safety Message/Plan), ICS-213 (General Message), and ICS-221 (Demobilization Check-Out), needed to assist with information collection and dissemination during an incident
- Describe the importance of a demobilization plan

Forms Overview

The forms presented in this lesson are supplemental forms designed to:

- Support information sharing for the ICS process they address
- Assist during the incident
- Serve as further documentation to support:
    - Development of the incident after-action report
    - Reimbursement/cost documentation
    - Incident timeline and history

The ICS supplemental forms discussed in this lesson are used to assist the Incident Management team in the management and documentation of incidents.

ICS-208: Safety Message/Plan

Purpose: The Safety Message/Plan (ICS-208) expands on the Safety Message and Site Safety Plan. It may be included as part of the IAP and is used to convey statements for safety messages, priorities, and key command emphasis/decisions/directions. These messages can include information such as known safety hazards and specific precautions to be observed during an operational period.

Preparation: The ICS-208 is an optional form that may be included and completed by the Safety Officer for the IAP.

Distribution: The ICS-208, if developed, will be reproduced with the IAP and given to all recipients as part of the IAP. All completed forms must be given to the Documentation Unit in the Planning Section.

ICS-213: General Message

Purpose: The General Message (ICS-213) is used by the incident personnel and dispatchers to record incoming messages that cannot be orally transmitted with accuracy to the intended recipients. The ICS-213 is also used by the Incident Command Post and other incident personnel to transmit messages (e.g., resource order, incident name change, other ICS coordination issues, etc.) to the Incident Communications Center for transmission via radio or telephone to the addressee(s). This form is used to send any message or notification to incident personnel who require hard-copy delivery.

Preparation: The ICS-213 may be initiated by any personnel on an incident.

Distribution: Upon completion, the ICS-213 may be delivered to the addressee and/or delivered to the Incident Communications Center for transmission.

Demobilization Plan Overview

Demobilization is the release and return of resources that are no longer required, and is a planned process. The Demobilization Check-Out (ICS-221) can be used in planning for demobilization.

A demobilization plan details the following:

- Specific responsibilities
- Release priorities
- Release procedures
- Checklists
- General information

How Demobilization Works

IC/UC: Approves resource orders and demobilization.

Operations Section: Identifies operational resources that are, or will be, in excess for the incident and prepares list for Demobilization Unit Leader.

<u>Planning Section</u>: Develops and implements the demobilization plan.

<u>Logistics Section</u>: Implements transportation inspection program and handles special transport needs.

<u>Finance/Administration Section</u>: Processes claims, time records, incident costs, and assists in release priorities.

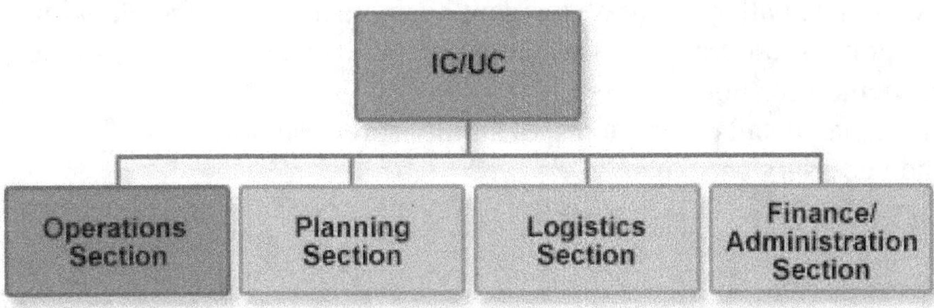

ICS-221: Demobilization Check-Out

Purpose: The Demobilization Check-Out (ICS-221) form ensures that resources checking out of the incident have completed all appropriate incident business, and provides the Planning Section documentation on resources released from the incident.

Preparation: The ICS-221 is initiated by the Planning Section, or a Demobilization Unit Leader if designated. The Demobilization Unit Leader completes the top portion of the form and checks the appropriate boxes in Block 6 that may need attention after the Resources Unit Leader has given written notification that the resource is no longer needed. The individual resource will have the appropriate overhead personnel sign off on any checked box(es) in Block 6 prior to release from the incident.

Distribution: After completion, the ICS-221 is returned to the Demobilization Unit Leader or the Planning Section. All completed forms must be given to the Documentation Unit in the Planning Section. Demobilizing personnel may request to retain a copy of the ICS-221.

Lesson Summary

- ICS-208: Safety Message/Plan – includes information such as known safety hazards and specific precautions to be observed during a given operational period
- ICS-213: General Message – used to record messages that cannot be transmitted orally or when a hard-copy delivery is required
- ICS-221: Demobilization Check-out - ensures that resources checking out of the incident have completed all appropriate incident business, provides the Planning Section information on resources released from the incident, and assists with the planning of the demobilization process
- A demobilization plan details specific responsibilities, release priorities, procedures, and necessary checklists

Lesson 7: Course Summary

Introduction

Welcome to Lesson 7, Course Summary and Final Examination. At the conclusion of this lesson, you will be able to:

- Summarize the IS-201 course, citing key components of the course

Course Summary

The ICS forms discussed in this course are valuable tools that can be used to:

- Gather and disseminate information
- Develop a common operational picture and situational awareness
- Provide a comprehensive understanding of incident status, intended objectives, and resource utilization
- Assist in building the IAP in conjunction with and supporting the planning process
- Account for all participants operating at the incident
- Ensure there is a legal and historical record of the event